High-Tech Science

HOW DOES WIFI WORK?

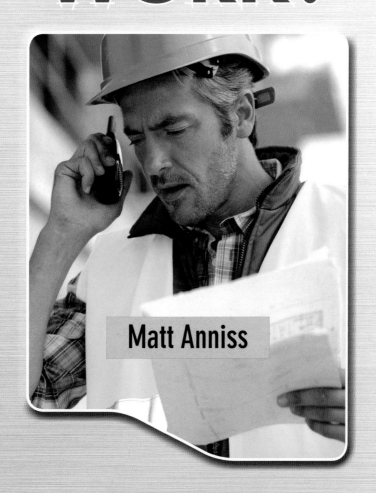

Matt Anniss

Gareth Stevens
Publishing

Please visit our website, www.garethstevens.com. For a free color catalog of all our high-quality books, call toll free 1-800-542-2595 or fax 1-877-542-2596.

Library of Congress Cataloging-in-Publication Data

Anniss, Matt.
How does wifi work? / by Matt Anniss.
 p. cm. — (High-tech science)
Includes index.
ISBN 978-1-4824-0400-5 (pbk.)
ISBN 978-1-4824-3311-1 (6-pack)
ISBN 978-1-4824-0399-2 (library binding)
1. Wireless communication systems — Juvenile literature. I. Anniss, Matt. II. Title.
TK5103.2 A56 2014
621.384—dc23

First Edition

Published in 2014 by
Gareth Stevens Publishing
111 East 14th Street, Suite 349
New York, NY 10003

© 2014 Gareth Stevens Publishing

Produced by Calcium, www.calciumcreative.co.uk
Designed by Simon Borrough
Edited by Sarah Eason and Jennifer Sanderson

Photo credits: Cover: Shutterstock: Takayuki. Inside: Dreamstime: Ilka Antonova 23, Aprescindere 29, Chrissuperseal 31, Sebastian Czapnik 39l, Edward Fielding 40, Konradbak 18, Andrei Malov 16, Zhanna Malinina 19r, Dimitar Marinov 28, Anna Martynova 20, Sergiy Mashchenko 15, Photomyeye 26, Pressureua 42, Andres Rodriguez 27, Jonathan Ross 17, Werner Stoffberg 44, Satayu Sengsomwong 22, Ralf Siemieniec 25, Sudheer K.s 24, Jozsef Szasz-fabian 21, Xiye 45t, Michael Zhang 3, 19l, Xi Zhang 45b; Shutterstock: 3Dstock 35, AL1962 14, Auremar 11, 41, Bagiuiani 37, R Carner 8, Creatista 32, Diego Cervo 7, Dean Drobot 12, Everett Collection 6, Brian A Jackson 5, Goodluz 1, 9, Oleksiy Mark 39r, Laschon Maximilian 13, Maxx-Studio 4, Mikeledray 30, Monkey Business Images 38, NatUlrich 36, Charles B. Ming Onn 33, William Perugini 43, Pressmaster 34, Roberaten 10.

Printed in the United States of America

CPSIA compliance information: Batch #CW14GS. For further information contact Gareth Stevens, New York, New York at 1-800-542-2595.

CONTENTS

Chapter One: How WiFi Works   4

Chapter Two: Wireless Networks   14

Chapter Three: Wireless Technology
    Through Time   24

Chapter Four: How People Use WiFi   34

Glossary   46

For More Information   47

Index   48

CHAPTER ONE:
HOW WIFI WORKS

Today, we know that we can turn on our laptops, tablets, and cell phones, and within seconds we will be connected to the Internet. Most of the time, we do not need to plug in cables or wires because there is a WiFi "hotspot" nearby. WiFi lets us surf the Web, watch videos, or listen to music without being at a fixed computer.

Connecting to the Internet on the move, using smartphones and laptops, is made possible by WiFi.

The way your television remote control works is very similar to the system that allows you to connect to the Internet wirelessly.

What Is WiFi?

WiFi, or wireless networking, is the process of connecting to the Internet without cables. The same information, or data, that would normally be sent to and from your computer or telephone using wires, is sent through the air instead. This is done using two or more electronic devices that are capable of sending and receiving data as radio waves.

Radio waves are invisible waves of energy, which are capable of carrying sound, pictures, and other forms of electronic information through the air over long distances (see page 6–7).

Wireless World

The technology used to develop the WiFi system that we use today is an advanced version of radio technology that has existed for more than 100 years. It is the same technology that is used to operate the remote control handsets of our televisions and home stereos. Car keys that allow drivers to lock and unlock their vehicles by pressing a button use a technology that is very similar to WiFi technology, too.

WHY WIFI?

The technology used to connect to the Internet wirelessly was invented in the 1980s. However, the term "WiFi" came into use only in 1999. It was invented to try to get more people to use the then-expensive technology. It certainly sounds better than the technology's official title, which is IEEE 802.11b Direct Sequence!

RADIO WAVES

To understand how WiFi works, you need to know a little more about radio waves and how they work. Radio waves are a form of electrical energy. They are created using a simple electrical process and can be used to send information, such as sound, moving pictures, and computer data, over long distances.

The system of searching for radio waves transmitted by a radio transmitter has not changed since radios were first invented.

Invisible Touch

We cannot see radio waves, but if we could, they would look like a continuous wavy line with several of peaks (the high points of the wave) and troughs (the low points of the wave). These peaks and troughs are exactly the same size.

Types of Radio Wave

There are many different types of radio wave. For example, microwaves are used for heating and cooking food in microwave ovens and for making and receiving cell phone calls. Infrared radio waves are used to operate remote control handsets. The radio waves used in wireless networking are called sine waves.

Long Waves, Short Distances

Sine waves are long waves, but they are weak. They are strong enough to travel only up to around 330 feet (100 m). However, because WiFi signals only have to travel short distances, using sine waves means the waves can carry a lot of information. This is why we can "stream" high-definition movies directly to our computers, tablets, or smartphones.

THE PROPERTIES OF SINE WAVES

There are large distances between the peaks and troughs of sine waves. This makes the waves perfect for sending information over long distances. However, this is possible only if the equipment that creates and sends the radio waves is very powerful (such as a large television or radio transmitter), otherwise they can send information only a short distance.

When you call someone, your cell phone communicates with the cellular network using a type of radio wave called a microwave.

TWO-WAY COMMUNICATION

For many years after the discovery of radio waves, scientists focused on sending, or broadcasting, radio signals over long distances. To do this, they invented powerful transmitters, called antennas. These signals could be picked up using a receiver device, such as a portable radio or a television aerial.

One-Way Communication

The system used to broadcast radio signals using a receiver is known as one-way communication. In this system, only one end of the link is communicating or broadcasting, while the other is simply receiving. Remote control handsets work using one-way communication—a television or stereo responds to the pressing of a button. A system called "two-way communication" allows us to send and receive radio waves at the same time.

When using one-way radio communication, the person on the other end of the radio must wait until the first person has finished speaking before he or she replies.

The walkie-talkie radio, which was more popular before the development of cell phones, is a good example of a two-way communication device.

Two's Company

The technology behind two-way communication is simple. All it requires are devices that are capable of sending and receiving radio waves. These devices can turn sound, pictures, or computer data into radio waves before sending them out into the world. They can also receive radio waves and turn them back into sound, pictures, or computer data.

The most basic example of this system in action is the walkie-talkie. A walkie-talkie is a small, handheld portable radio that allows people to talk to each other over short distances.

TWO-WAY WIFI

Wireless networking used in computer WiFi connections is a great example of two-way communication. When you are connected to the Internet using WiFi, your computer, tablet, or smartphone is constantly sending and receiving data in the form of radio waves.

HITTING THE RIGHT FREQUENCY

From WiFi computer networking and remote control handsets to walkie-talkie radios and smartphones, all two-way wireless devices that use radio waves send and receive information in very similar ways. How do all these devices successfully communicate given the number of wireless devices in use today?

The Radio Spectrum

Light, sound, and electrical signals all travel around the world and the universe as waves. Together, these invisible forms of energy make up the electromagnetic spectrum. The part of the spectrum that can be used by radio waves is called the radio spectrum.

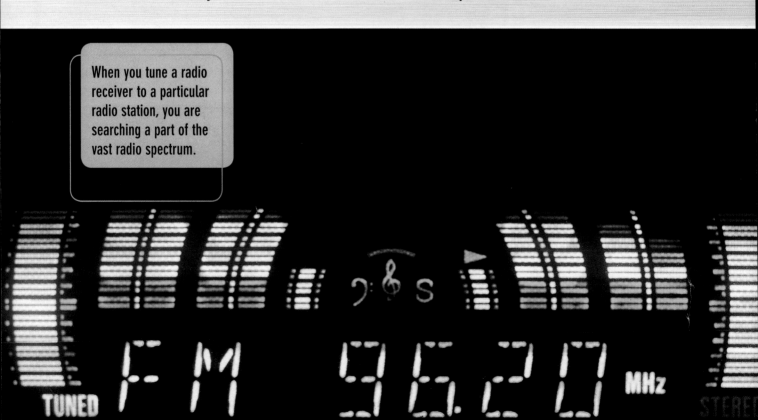

When you tune a radio receiver to a particular radio station, you are searching a part of the vast radio spectrum.

TUNED   FM   96.20   MHz   STERE

To ensure that all systems that use radio waves are accommodated in the radio spectrum, each is given its own narrow space, or frequency. By law, devices must send (and receive, if they are capable of doing this) radio waves only on their own frequency.

Frequency Bands

There are a vast amount of frequencies within the radio spectrum, but the spectrum is not infinite. At some point, there will be no space left for new systems. However, as yet, we have not run out of space because different forms of technology broadcast on different frequencies. For example, AM radio is broadcast from 535 kilohertz to 1,700 kilohertz (thousands of radio waves per second). FM radio stations broadcast in a range of frequencies between 88 and 108 megahertz (millions of radio waves per second). WiFi devices communicate on frequencies between 2.4 and 5 gigahertz (billions of radio waves per second).

HOPPING AROUND

Many modern WiFi devices use a system called "frequency hopping" to guarantee the user a good signal. This means that the device can flick between up to three different radio frequencies to ensure that the connection does not drop.

By using frequency hopping, WiFi systems can guarantee both a fast and reliable Internet connection.

WIRELESS INTERNET

The process used by WiFi devices to connect to the Internet is similar to that used by two-way radios. However, instead of sound being turned into radio waves and back again, it is computer data.

Getting Connected

To create a connection to the Internet, your WiFi-enabled device, for example a laptop, tablet computer, or smartphone, needs to communicate with another device, called a wireless router. The wireless router is connected to the Internet using a special kind of wire called an Ethernet cable.

When you turn on a tablet computer, such as an iPad, it will automatically try to connect to the nearest WiFi network.

Wireless Adapters

When you switch on your laptop, tablet, or smartphone, it attempts to connect to the Internet through the router. It does this using a device called a wireless adapter. This is a tiny antenna capable of turning instructions in the form of computer data (for example, a request to send an email) into a radio signal.

WORKING OVERTIME

When you are listening to music over the Internet using WiFi, your computer is constantly communicating with the wireless router. Both devices are able to send and receive huge amounts of data very quickly, roughly enough to download a 4 minute long MP3 in less than 10 seconds.

Quick Process

The router receives this signal, turns it back into computer data, and acts on the instructions. Once it has done this, it then turns the computer data back into radio waves, which it sends to your WiFi device. The device's wireless adapter receives the signal and turns it back into computer data. This whole process takes only a fraction of a second.

4

PWR   SYS   WLAN   WAN

Wireless routers like this one connect wireless devices to the network that carries computer data around the world.

CHAPTER TWO:
WIRELESS NETWORKS

Connecting to the Internet using WiFi is made possible not just by radio waves and wireless adapters, but also by a vast global network of underground cables. Without these cables, we would not be able to connect to the Internet on the move.

The Importance of Wires and Cables

If you take a look at the back of a wireless router, you will notice a thick, rubber-coated cable plugged in to it. This is an Ethernet cable. This cable is the wireless router's gateway to the vast network of underground communications cables that carry computer data around the world.

These underground communications cables crisscross neighborhoods, towns, cities, states, countries, and even oceans. Together they form the wide area network. Without the wide area network, the Internet would not work.

Ethernet cables provide a link between a WiFi router and the hidden cables that carry computer data all around the world.

Servers like these are used to store information such as popular websites.

Network Basics

The wide area network joins together millions of computers around the world. Every website is "hosted" on a computer somewhere in the world, usually a large storage computer called a server. When you type in a website address and press the return key, your computer, tablet, or smartphone sends a request for access to the host computer. Even when you connect wirelessly using a router, this request is sent down cables across the wide area network, until it reaches its destination. The response to your request will come back down the same cables, be turned into radio waves by your wireless router, and is then beamed through the air to your device.

HIGH-SPEED CABLES

Today's underground cables use a system called fiber optics. In this system, data is turned into pulses of light, which can be beamed down the cables at super-fast speeds. It can take just a few hundredths of a second for a fiber-optic signal to travel from one side of the world to the other.

WIRELESS LOCAL AREA NETWORKS

The wide area network that carries computer data around the world is actually a collection of lots of smaller networks. The smallest of these are called local area networks. These are the networks used in homes, schools, colleges, and offices.

Before WiFi, the only way for many devices in the same place to connect to the Internet was by using Ethernet cables.

What Is a Local Area Network?

A local area network allows several computers, and other electronic devices, to share a single connection to the Internet. Before wireless technology, the computers in a local area network would be connected to a single Internet router using Ethernet cables.

Wireless Local Area Network

Today, most local area networks operate using wireless technology. Using a wireless router, the devices can share the same Internet connection without plugging into cables. This is what is known as a wireless local area network, or WLAN.

Overload

Using a WLAN, it is possible for several different wireless devices to connect to the Internet at the same time. This is because the wireless router is capable of communicating with many different devices at the same time. However, the router can send and receive only a certain amount of data at any given time. This is why the Internet can sometimes seem slow at busy periods of the day.

Many schools and colleges set up WLANs to allow students to connect to the Internet.

WIRELESS WONDER

In addition to connecting to the Internet, WLANs have other uses. Once you have set up a WLAN in your home, you could use it to transfer documents and files between different computers in the same WLAN, or access a shared music collection stored on a shared computer.

HOTSPOTS

If you could connect only to your own WLAN, wireless technology would be of limited use. However, there are now WiFi "hotspots" all over towns and cities, from libraries and restaurants to airports and railroad stations, making it possible to connect to the Internet almost anywhere you go.

WiFi hotspots allow friends to surf the Web while meeting at a local coffee shop or restaurant.

How Hotspots Work

WiFi hotspots exist when the owners of a business or building offer access to their wireless router, often free of charge. Computer, tablet, and smartphone users can then connect to the Internet during their time in that building or public space.

Normally, buildings or businesses that offer a WiFi hotspot service advertise the fact. Sometimes, you will need to enter a password to gain access to the network, but this is usually advertised, too.

PERSONAL HOTSPOT

If you or someone you know has an iPhone, you can create your own hotspot. To do this, you will need to turn on the "personal hotspot" option in the "preferences" section. When this is turned on, the iPhone will become a wireless router. You can then share your iPhone's wireless connection with other devices, such as a laptop or iPad. This is especially convenient if you are out and about and need access to the Internet.

Free and Easy

Each WiFi hotspot is, in fact, a WLAN, just like the one you may have at home or school. The difference is that the people who own the network allow many different people to use it. They pay the cost of the Internet connection so you do not have to. You would not be quite so pleased if people were using your home WLAN for free, rather than paying for their own!

Most airports have WiFi hotspots, which are shown by various signs like this one. This means travelers can connect to the Internet while they wait to board flights.

NETWORK SECURITY

If you are using a wireless network, it is very important that you protect yourself when working online. This means taking security measures to make sure that criminals cannot get hold of our personal information. By adding password protection to your WLAN, people will need to correctly enter a password before they can connect to your home WLAN.

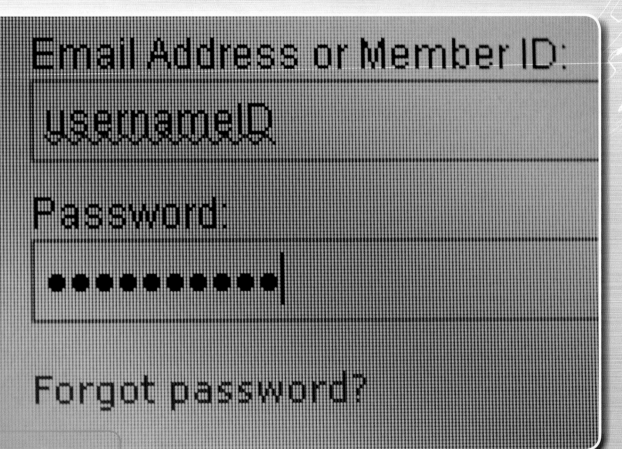

Using security measures, such as password protection, stops people from accessing your home WiFi connection without your permission.

Password Protection

Early wireless routers were not very secure, and users complained to the manufacturers that their built-in security systems were not good enough. Thanks to years of development, wireless routers are now very secure. They use a number of systems to protect their connections from being hijacked by criminals.

WPA2

The most widely used system to protect WLANs is called WiFi Protected Access 2, or WPA2. To connect to a WLAN that is protected by WPA2, you need to enter a password. Once you do this, you will be granted access. As there is an almost infinite number of possible passwords, this makes it a lot harder for criminals to "hack" into your WiFi network.

Controlling Access

Another popular WiFi security system is called Media Access Control (MAC). Every computer in the world has a unique MAC address. If you know the MAC address of your computer, and that of other users of your WLAN, you can get your router to grant access only to these computers.

PIGGYBACKING

The process of hopping between free WiFi networks that are not password protected is called "piggybacking." Some computer users do this so that they do not have to pay for their own Internet connection.

Without security measures, hackers could use your WiFi connection to access personal information from your computer.

DIRECT WIRELESS NETWORKS

The technology that allows electronic devices to send and receive data as radio waves has more uses than simply connecting to the Internet. It is now possible for some electronic devices to communicate between each other directly, without the need to set up a WLAN.

Handheld barcode scanners, as found in large homeware stores, are a good example of direct wireless technology at work.

Ad Hoc Action

Ad hoc WiFi transmission is when two electronic devices communicate directly using wireless technology. One of the most popular uses of this is in the "wireless ad hoc network" mode offered by handheld game consoles such as the Nintendo DS and PlayStation Portable (PSP). This mode allows gamers in the same room to play networked games against each other. For ad hoc wireless transmission to work, each handheld console must wirelessly connect to the others using its built-in wireless adapter.

Bluetooth

Another form of direct wireless networking is a system called Bluetooth. Bluetooth was invented in the 1990s to allow electronic devices, such as cell phones, laptops, and digital cameras to communicate with each other. Like WiFi, Bluetooth uses radio waves to send and receive data. However, the radio waves it uses are much shorter than those used in WiFi, so connections can only take place between devices that are a few feet apart.

This driver's earpiece is connected to his cell phone wirelessly, using Bluetooth technology.

HANDS FREE

One of the most popular uses of Bluetooth technology is the hands-free headsets worn by drivers. When the driver's cell phone rings, he or she presses a button on the headset to answer the phone. Using radio waves, the phone then transfers the call to and from the headset via Bluetooth.

CHAPTER THREE:
WIRELESS TECHNOLOGY THROUGH TIME

The wireless technology that makes so much difference to our lives today is the result of more than 100 years of research and development. Without certain key discoveries, today's super-fast WiFi connections would not be possible.

Wireless Waves

The development of wireless technology began in 1876, when a German scientist named Heinrich Rudolf Hertz proved the existence of radio waves. However, Hertz thought his discovery had little merit. He is reported to have said: "Wireless waves will not have any practical application."

Tesla's Work

Hertz could not have been more wrong! By 1892, a Croatian scientist named Nikola Tesla had demonstrated that radio waves could be transmitted. Tesla had figured out that it was possible to artificially create and send radio waves out into the world.

Founding Father

Tesla is the founding father of wireless technology. His wireless telegraphy system later became the basis of radio broadcasting. In 1898, Tesla wowed crowds in Madison Square Garden, New York, by demonstrating the world's first radio-controlled boat. Remote controlled toy cars, boats, and airplanes used today are based on the system Tesla invented.

Nearly 100 years after the first US radio stations started broadcasting, millions of people around the world listen to radio broadcasts every day.

To make sure his radio broadcasts could be heard on the other side of the Atlantic Ocean, Marconi built a radio transmitter like this one.

The Radio Revolution

In 1901, long-range radio broadcasting arrived. With money from US investors, including inventor Thomas Edison, Italian scientist Guglielmo Marconi sent the first radio transmission across the Atlantic Ocean. Using powerful radio transmitters in Newfoundland and Ireland, he proved that radio waves could be used to send sound over thousands of miles.

Within 25 years, almost every home in the United States had a radio receiver. Radio stations, which broadcasted music, talk, and drama, appeared all over the world to entertain listeners.

RADAR

Heinrich Rudolph Hertz did not only discover that radio waves could be transmitted, but he also discovered that they can be reflected when they hit solid objects in their path.

Radio Detection and Ranging

During the 1930s and early 1940s, governments around the world conducted secret experiments to see if Hertz's discovery, made some 50 years earlier, could be used to warn of attacks from the air. The system they developed became known as radar, which is short for Radio Detection And Ranging.

Radar receivers are used by the military to track the movement of airplanes and missiles high in the sky.

All modern aircraft use radar systems to help keep track of where they are in the sky, and to help keep them clear of other aircraft.

RADAR TODAY

Today, air traffic controllers use radar to track the position of planes in the sky as they crisscross the world. Radar is also used to keep track of the world's weather systems. The United States boasts a vast network of radar stations, which are used to predict the movements of dangerous storms. This means people can be warned of an approaching storm and the necessary precautions can be taken.

How Radar Works

The principles behind radar are simple. A powerful transmitter pointed toward the sky sends out a continuous stream of radio waves. When the radio waves hit a solid object, they are reflected, or scattered, in many directions. Some bounce back toward the transmitter. By placing a receiver device close to the transmitter, it is possible to figure out the exact position in the sky of the object that was hit.

War Heroes

Radar systems were first put into use in World War II (1939–1945), when they helped the British and US forces to defeat the Germans. By detecting overhead planes, the two countries' air forces could send up their own planes to shoot down the German counterparts. Since then, the use of radar has become widespread and the system is no longer used by the military alone.

SPACE SATELLITES

The discovery that radio waves could travel long distances and be reflected back toward the point of their origin, has led to the development of even more cutting-edge technology in the last 50 years.

Stargazing

One of the most significant inventions is radio astronomy. Radio astronomy is based on the principle that all objects transmit energy in the form of radio waves.

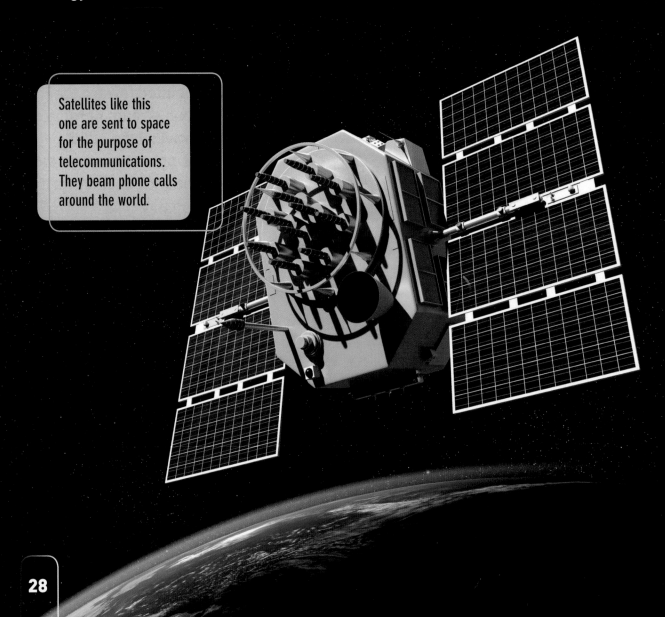

Satellites like this one are sent to space for the purpose of telecommunications. They beam phone calls around the world.

There are thousands of objects in space. These include planets, galaxies, and satellites. All of these objects, even those that are millions of miles away, send out radio waves. Astronomers use large radio antennas that are powerful enough to receive their signals to find out where in the sky these objects are.

Satellite television receivers, like this dish on the roof of a house, pick up radio waves broadcast from satellites above Earth.

Satellite Serenade

Another use of radio waves developed in the last 50 years is satellite technology. Scientists realized that by placing reflective objects, known as satellites, in set points above Earth, they could bounce radio waves off them and back toward our planet. This technology has several applications, including satellite television.

Satellite Television

In order for satellite television to work, pictures are turned into radio waves, and beamed to a satellite in space. The satellite then sends the radio waves back toward Earth, where they are picked up by receivers (satellite dishes) and turned back into television pictures.

CELL PHONE TECHNOLOGY

Although satellite technology has improved our lives and radio astronomy has increased our understanding of the universe, neither technology has affected our lives quite as much as cell phone technology, which allows us to communicate wherever we are in the world. Today, it is thought that there are 7 billion cell phones connected.

Wave Power

Cell phones use radio waves to send and receive information, or data. Each time you make or receive a call on a cell phone or a smartphone, the data is routed around the world using a network of masts, which are capable of sending and receiving radio waves, and satellites positioned high above Earth.

Early cell phones from the 1970s and 1980s were so large that they had to be carried around in a bag.

The Cell Phone Network

The global cell phone, or cellular, network is divided into a series of small grids, or cells. Each cell has its own mast, and each mast is given its own unique radio frequency to send and receive calls. As users pass from one cell to the next, their phone automatically detects the change and tunes in to the new frequency.

Superfast Connections

Today, the masts that make up the cell phone network, and the phones that use them, are capable of sending much more data than radio waves. You can connect to the Internet, watch movies, and listen to live radio over the network.

Cell phone masts, such as the one above, are a familiar sight in many towns and cities. They are often placed on the top of tall buildings.

THE 4G NETWORK

The third generation (3G) and fourth generation (4G) cell phone networks we use today can send and receive huge amounts of computer data very quickly. The 4G network gives you a connection that is 30 times faster than a 3G connection—in fact, 4G is almost as fast as WiFi.

THE DAWN OF WIRELESS INTERNET

When computer networking became popular in the late 1980s, scientists began developing wireless connections using radio waves. Yet, however hard they tried, they could not create a clear signal and a strong connection.

Finding the Solution

When they travel, radio waves bounce off solid objects. To make wireless networking possible, scientists would have to create a system where a good proportion of radio waves reached their intended destination.

WiFi routers send and receive thousands of radio waves a second, so many people can connect to the Internet on their phones at the same time.

If you cannot connect to the Internet using a WiFi router, it is possible to connect over the cell phone network instead, using a device called a dongle (see page 37).

WHEN WiFi FAILS

Despite O'Sullivan's discovery, WiFi is still not perfect. Wireless routers have a range of up to about 330 feet (100 m), but users will usually receive a strong signal only if they are within 165 feet (50 m) of the router. The signal will also be weaker if there are objects in the way.

Loud and Clear

In 1992, Australian radio astronomer John O'Sullivan made a significant breakthrough. He discovered that if you split the radio signal into a vast number of radio waves, enough waves would get through to ensure a clear signal and a good connection.

Huge Growth

O'Sullivan and his research team created a wireless adapter that could be included in laptops and wireless routers. It went on sale to computer manufacturers in 2000, and within 6 years more than 100 million people were regularly using WiFi. Today, wireless adapters come as standard in almost all computers, smartphones, and tablets, as well as other devices such as game consoles. In just more than 20 years, WiFi has become the standard way of connecting to the Internet.

CHAPTER FOUR:
HOW PEOPLE USE WIFI

The boom in wireless technology in the last few years, and in particular WiFi Internet, has changed the way we live our lives. Whether we are at home, out and about, or even on vacation, WiFi has made a hugely dramatic difference to our daily lives.

WiFi World

If you think about some of the ways people use a computer or laptop, tablet, or smartphone, and where they use the these devices, you will quickly realize just how much people rely on wireless Internet connections.

In an average day, people may update their status on social networking site, such as Facebook, post something on Twitter, upload pictures of themselves and friends to sites such as Instagram or Flickr, or watch videos on YouTube. Whichever device people use, and wherever they do this, all these activities are only possible thanks to WiFi.

Using tablets to access social networks has become possible thanks to WiFi. Users can chat to friends or upload photos while they are out and about.

Always Connected

As a result of the wireless network, people are almost always connected. Smartphones will automatically connect to any WiFI network that the phone recognizes. This is usually one that is free, or one that people have previously connected to by entering a password. If there is no WiFi network available, people can connect to the Internet over the cellular cell phone network instead. Almost anywhere people are in the United States, they can connect to the Internet at any time of day.

The map applications on smartphones use GPS to figure out where you are and to give you directions to a destination.

LOCATION, LOCATION

Have you ever wondered how your smartphone knows where you are in the world, and how people can add their location to Facebook or Twitter posts? A smartphone does this by accessing the Global Positioning System (GPS). The GPS is a network of satellites high above Earth that can accurately locate the position of any GPS-enabled device.

DOING BUSINESS

WiFi has changed the way people work. Business people no longer have to be based in an office building with wired access to the Internet. Now people can do business on the move, using their laptops, tablet computers, and smartphones.

On the Move

Business people who have to travel a lot are well served by the wireless world. Today, most major railroad stations and airports offer WiFi access. WiFi also comes as standard at many hotels and an increasing number of coffee shops, restaurants, and bars offer free WiFi to their customers. As long as people have a laptop or a smartphone, they can work almost anywhere in the world.

With a laptop computer and an Internet enabled smartphone, people can take their work with them on the train.

Thanks to apps people can do almost everything on the move, from shopping and emailing to setting up business meetings.

DISCOVERING DONGLES

Many cell phone providers also sell a device called a dongle. A dongle allows laptop users to connect to the Internet using the cellular network. Using them is very simple. All that is required is to plug the dongle into the USB port of a laptop, wait until the software loads and click on "connect." As long as the user can get cell phone reception, they will be able to connect to the Internet.

Apps On the Go

Many smart applications, or apps, have been developed to make doing business easier. For example, many banks now offer their customers apps that allow them to manage their money on their phones, wherever they are in the world. Some stores also can now take credit card payments using wireless card readers. These handheld devices communicate with the customer's bank using a secure WiFi connection.

CHANGING TELEVISION

Wireless technology is also changing the world of television, and specifically how we watch it. Families once gathered together to watch television. Today, each family member can watch what they want, when they want.

Television Anytime

Thanks to the invention of personal television recorder boxes such as TiVo, people can now watch their favorite programs at a time that suits them. This technology may seem modern, but today even greater cutting-edge television technologies are available.

Television Apps

Many satellite and cable television companies have smartphone apps. These allow users to tell their set-top box to record a program, even if they are thousands of miles away from home. There are also apps that allow you to turn your smartphone into a remote control to change channels using your WLAN.

Thanks to "connected television" services such as TiVo, we can now watch any program at any time.

Television Anywhere

The speed of WiFi Internet connections has also led to a rise in the popularity of "television on demand" services. These are either websites, such as YouTube, or apps, such as NBC On Demand, which allow you to watch programs on your laptop, smartphone, game console, or tablet. You can use these services anywhere, as long as you have a good WiFi connection.

Using a WiFi connection, you can access the Internet through your television.

"Streaming" websites, such as YouTube, have revolutionized the way we watch television by allowing us to see our favorite shows on many different electronic devices.

STREAM ON

It is now possible to create your own mini "home television network" using your computer and WLAN. Services such as iTunes and Apple television allow users to store movies and television episodes on one computer, and then transmit, or stream, the pictures to other computers, tablets, and smartphones that are connected to the WLAN.

PLAYING GAMES

It is not only the invention of online gaming that has changed the way people play games. Wireless technology has also made playing computer games a much more energetic and athletic activity.

Game consoles, such as the Nintendo Wii, use wireless technology to make playing games a better experience.

Wireless Playtime

Two of the most popular game consoles of recent years, the Wii and the Xbox 360, owe much of their popularity to the wireless technology in each machine.

Both consoles contain wireless adapters to connect to the Internet. Both offer players the chance to play networked games against opponents from all over the world, using the Internet. Both consoles use wireless controllers that feature motion sensors. Motion sensors pick up on a player's movement and react accordingly.

Using WiFi, people in the same room can play games against each other using two or more wireless devices.

HOW DO MOTION SENSORS WORK?

Motion sensors work by sending and receiving waves of invisible light, known as infrared light. In the case of game consoles, the base unit transmits waves of light, while the remote control receives them. Every time the remote detects a wave of light, it sends back the information to the base unit, using radio waves. It then updates the game on screen.

Wireless Mode

It is not just game consoles that have embraced the world of WiFi gaming. Many games designed for smartphones and tablet computers feature wireless game modes. These allow two or more users to play multiplayer games over their home WLAN. Users do not need to connect to the Internet to play, because the wireless router acts as a middle man between two phones, laptops, or tablet computers.

WIRELESS WORLD

The advances in wireless technology in recent years have made amazing innovations possible, several that some thought would never be possible.

Sound and Pictures

One of the biggest advances is video calling, which has been made popular by software applications such as Skype and Apple's Facetime. These applications allow you to make live video calls to people, or leave video messages, either over a WiFi Internet connection or the cell phone network. To use these applications, all you need is a smartphone, a tablet computer, or a laptop with an built-in webcam.

Video calling helps us keep in touch with loved ones, even if they live thousands of miles away.

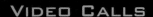

VIDEO CALLS

Video calls work because the sound from the phone's microphone and the moving pictures from its camera are turned into computer data. This data is then turned into radio waves that are sent to the WiFi router or cell phone network. The process also works in reverse, so you can watch and hear the other person as you talk.

Music on My Mind

The development of superfast wireless connections has also made listening to music on the move much easier. Now, you can stream live radio or DJ mixes on your smartphone or tablet computer, download new albums in a matter of seconds, and even broadcast your own radio shows from the comfort of your home.

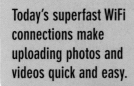

Today's superfast WiFi connections make uploading photos and videos quick and easy.

Live Television

If you have a WiFi connection, you can also watch live television, including sports events, wherever you are. Many sports channels, such as Fox Sports and ESPN, offer special Internet subscriptions. These allow you to pay to watch the channel on your laptop, desktop computer, or tablet. Some channels even allow you to choose which match you watch when a number of events start at the same time.

WIFI WONDERS

WiFi as we know it today did not exist 20 years ago. Now, it enhances our lives by keeping us connected to the world through the Internet 24 hours a day. Whether we want to play games, chat with friends, share photos, manage our money, or choose what television programs or movies to watch, WiFi allows us to do it.

The Need for Speed

The pace of this change has almost been as fast as the fiber-optic cables that carry computer data around the world at the speed of light. It is the speed of the connection more than the invention of WiFi technology that has enabled our wireless world. The speed of the connection between your computer and wireless router is important, but without a quick Internet connection, it would be irrelevant. Fast Internet means fast WiFI, and ultimately this enables all of the activities we have come to expect, such as quickly uploading pictures and watching videos online.

In today's wireless age, even road signs can be connected to the world using WiFi.

Given how easy it is to connect to the Internet wirelessly, think how different your life would be without WiFi!

In just over 100 years, WiFi has been added to telephone booths. Where will we be in another 100 years?

More to Come

WiFi is still a new technology. While the power of radio waves has been used for more than 100 years, it is only since 2000 that we have enjoyed wireless Internet connections. Like any new technology, WiFi is always developing. In years to come, we will probably be able to send more computer data at a quicker pace than we do today. That means even better quality videos and music that will stream even faster. Better, faster connections will also mean smartphone apps that push the technology to its very limits.

45

GLOSSARY

aerial a piece of electronic equipment capable of receiving radio waves

antennas pieces of electronic equipment capable of receiving radio waves

apps short for application software. These programs tell a computer or other electronic device to do something.

Bluetooth a system created to allow cell phones and other devices to communicate with each other without the need for a wireless network

computer data information sent and received by computers or similar electronic devices

dongle a device that connects users to the Internet over the cell phone network rather than a wireless network

download the process of transferring something from the Internet onto your personal computer or smartphone

Ethernet cable a type of cable used for connecting or networking computers

fiber-optic cables cables made up of many long, thin strands of plastic or glass that turn information into pulses of light, rather than electrical signals

Internet the network of smaller computer networks that join together to form one single global network

radio astronomy the process of searching the universe using radio waves

radio waves invisible waves of energy that can pass through the air. Radio waves are used to transmit computer data, sound, and pictures.

smartphones cell phones with additional computing power

software a computer application or program designed to do a specific task, for example, send email, edit photos, or record music

tablets touchscreen computers, such as iPads

transmit to send information

transmitter something that transmits information, often in the form of radio waves or electrical signals

upload the process of transferring something from your computer, smartphone, or tablet to a website or Internet server

USB short for universal serial bus, which is a system for connecting electronic equipment to a computer

webcam a small video camera that connects to your computer and allows you to send and receive video messages or record short movies on your computer

wireless technology that allows the exchange of information, or communication between people, but does not require traditional cables or wires

wireless router a device that acts as a gateway between WiFi devices and the Internet

WLAN short for wireless local area network, or the combination of a wireless router and WiFi-enabled devices that allows you to connect to the Internet wirelessly

FOR MORE INFORMATION

Books

Firestone, Mary. *Cool Science: Wireless Technology*. Minneapolis, MN: Lerner Publications, 2008.

Hough, John R. *From Wireless to Radio*. Suffolk, UK: Abramis Academic Publishing, 2008.

Rand, Casey. *The Science Behind… Communication*. Mankato, MN: Heinemann-Raintree, 2012.

Websites

Find out more about how WiFi works at:
www.wireless-home-network-made-easy.com/wifi-technology.html

For information on radio waves and how they work, take a look at NASA's Mission Science website:
missionscience.nasa.gov/ems/05_radiowaves.html

If you have enjoyed reading this book, check out this website to find out more about the latest technology at:
www.sciencenewsforkids.org

INDEX

3G (third generation) 31
4G (fourth generation) 31

ad hoc wireless network 22
applications (apps) 35, 37, 38, 39,
    42, 45

Bluetooth 23

cell phone networks 31, 33, 35, 42, 43
cell phones 4, 7, 9, 23, 30–31, 37
computer networking 10, 32

dongles 33, 37

electromagnetic spectrum 10
Ethernet cables 12, 14, 16

fiber optics 15, 44
frequency hopping 11

game consoles 22, 33, 39, 40–41
gigahertz 11
GPS 35

Hertz, Heinrich Rudolph 24, 26

infrared 7, 41
Internet 4, 5, 9, 11, 12–13, 14, 16, 17, 18, 19,
    21, 22, 31, 32–33, 34, 35, 36, 37, 39, 41, 42,
    44, 45

kilohertz 11

local area networks 16

Marconi, Guglielmo 25
megahertz 11

passwords 18, 20, 21, 35
piggybacking 21

radar 26–27
radio
    radio astronomy 28–29, 30
    radio frequency 10–11, 31
    radio receivers 8, 10, 25, 27, 29
    radio signal 8, 13, 25, 33
    radio spectrum 10, 11
    radio transmitter 6, 7, 25, 27
    radio waves 5, 6–7, 8, 9, 10, 11, 12, 13, 14,
        15, 22, 23, 24, 25, 26, 27, 28, 29, 30, 31,
        32, 33, 41, 43, 45

satellites 28–29, 30, 35, 38
smartphones 7, 9, 10, 12, 13, 15, 18, 30, 33,
    34, 35, 36, 38, 39, 41, 42, 43, 45

television 5, 7, 8, 29, 38–39, 43, 44
Tesla, Nikola 24

video calls 42, 43

wide area network 14, 15, 16
WiFi hotspots 4, 18–19
WiFi Protected Access 2 (WPA2) 21
wireless adapters 13, 14, 22, 33, 41
wireless routers 12, 13, 14, 15, 17, 18, 19, 20,
    21, 32, 33, 41, 43, 44
WLAN (wireless local area network) 17, 18,
    19, 20, 21, 22, 38, 39, 41